The Lost Colony of Roanoke

WRITTEN BY

JEAN FRITZ

ILLUSTRATED BY

HUDSON TALBOTT

G. P. Putnam's Sons ♦ New York

THE NEW WORLD

Menatonon

Manteo

Wingina

Powhatan

1ST VOYAGE
1 ship, 32 men

Sir Richard Grenville

2ND VOYAGE
7 ships, 500 men

Ralph Lane

the Dares

3RD VOYAGE
3 ships, 87 men, 17 women, 11 children

4TH VOYAGE
2 ships

Philip Amadas

Arthur Barlow

John White

Thomas Hariot

Queen Elizabeth

April 27, 1584

April 9, 1585

of Great Britain

April 26, 1587

John White

March 20, 1590

Sir Walter Raleigh
in charge of British
colonization of
America

Simon Fernandez

ATLANTIC
OCEAN

Sir Francis Drake shows up by chance Summer, 1586

John White

The Roanoke Voyages

1584-1590

To Sabra Woolley,
who started me out on my journey to the Lost Colony. —J. F.

To the indigenous people of America,
with my prayer for forgiveness and healing. —H. T.

Text copyright © 2004 by Jean Fritz.
Illustrations copyright © 2004 by Hudson Talbott.
All rights reserved. This book, or parts thereof, may not be reproduced in any form
without permission in writing from the publisher, G. P. Putnam's Sons, a division of
Penguin Young Readers Group, 345 Hudson Street, New York, NY 10014.
G. P. Putnam's Sons, Reg. U.S. Pat. & Tm. Off. The scanning, uploading and distribution of this
book via the Internet or via any other means without the permission of the publisher is illegal and
punishable by law. Please purchase only authorized electronic editions, and do not participate in or
encourage electronic piracy of copyrighted materials. Your support of the author's rights is appreciated.
Published simultaneously in Canada. Manufactured in China by RR Donnelley Asia Printing Solutions Ltd.
Conceptual design by Hudson Talbott.
Typography by Cecilia Yung and Gunta Alexander. Text set in Trump Mediaeval.
The art was done in watercolor on Arches 140 lb. hot-press paper.

Library of Congress Cataloging-in-Publication Data
Fritz, Jean.   The Lost Colony of Roanoke / Jean Fritz ; illustrated by Hudson Talbott.   p. cm.
Summary: Describes the English colony of Roanoke, which was founded in 1585, and discusses
the mystery of its disappearance. 1. Roanoke Colony—Juvenile literature.
2. Roanoke Island (N.C.)—History—16th century—Juvenile literature. [1. Roanoke Colony.
2. Roanoke Island (N.C.)—History—16th century.] I. Talbott, Hudson, ill. II. Title.
F229 .F78 2004   975.6'175—dc21   2002152000   ISBN 978-0-399-24027-0
13

Author's Note

The best part of writing a book set in history is doing the research. And it is for the considerable help I received in preparing and writing this book that I am grateful. When I heard that an archaeological team was digging at Cape Hatteras in search of clues from the Lost Colony, I knew I wanted to be there. I called a friend in Washington, Sabra Woolley, an anthropologist, and asked if she wanted to go on a dig. "When do we leave?" she asked.

We left the next day and when we found the site, Sabra waded through the overgrowth of tall grass to inform the archaeologist, Dr. David Phelps, that she had a friend in the car in a wheelchair who was interested in the Lost Colony. Dr. Phelps instructed two young men in his team to carry me and the wheelchair to where the digging was taking place. I knew I wouldn't be able to dig, but I had a close-up view of the activity and I was allowed to sieve the sand that was being removed to make sure no artifacts were passed over. It was a perfect way to enter a four-hundred-year-old mystery.

Further along in my research, another friend, Sandra Garrison, took me for a day to Robeson County, North Carolina, where I talked to Lumbees, had dinner with Bruce Barton, an expert on Lumbee history, and explored the extensive archives of the University of North Carolina at Pembroke.

My gratitude for help extends beyond my research to the time I had to confront my temperamental computer. I am particularly grateful to Bobby Stutz, who on short notice typed up the final version of the manuscript. And to his parents, who helped me out of many pitfalls. Not least, I thank my daughter, Andrea, for her unfailing moral support.

Finally I am indebted to Dr. David Phelps, who not only allowed me a place on the edge of his dig but who read my completed manuscript to check its accuracy. As always, I thank my editor, Margaret Frith, for her encouragement, her critical eye, and her patience.

Jean Fritz

Looking

In the 1500s, when America was still a newfound land, every country wanted a piece of it. The Spanish were grabbing it up as fast as they could. They settled on a piece of leftover land that jutted out from North America. They called it Florida and claimed that it ran up the coast all the way to a big river (which would later be called the Hudson River).

The sails of Spanish ships dotted the sea like giant handkerchiefs blowing in the wind. English sails were there too, chasing the Spanish ships, for although the English weren't ready to settle yet, they did want the treasure that the Spanish were finding—gold, silver, hides, pepper, cloves, sugar, ivory. And pearls. Their queen was crazy about pearls.

The queen of England was Elizabeth, and there were two things that she didn't want: a war with Spain and a husband. Still, there were plenty of men who liked to hang out at the queen's court. Her favorite was Walter Raleigh. He was six feet tall, handsome, wore elegant clothes, and wrote love poems. Besides, he made Elizabeth feel queenly.

Once when they were out walking, they came to a huge mud puddle. And what did Walter do? He whipped off his elegant coat and flung it over the puddle. Of course his coat was ruined, but the queen's feet stayed dry.

What Walter really wanted to do was to play a part in settling this New World. First, he'd have to find out what it was like. For all he knew, the place might be a mess of mud puddles.

Philip Amadas

Arthur Barlow

So he asked his friend Dr. John Dee, who had a "show stone" that looked into the future. (He also had a beard so long, he could have sat on it if it had been on the other side of his head.) The stone said that if they went halfway up the coast, above where the Spanish were, they would find a long cape with islands hiding behind it. They could settle on one of them (later to be called Roanoke).

So Walter asked Philip Amadas and Arthur Barlow to go there and check it out. What kind of trees grew there? Walter asked. What kind of plants? What were the people like? Was there treasure?

Philip and Arthur left England on April 27, 1584, and returned in September, bubbling over with good news.

The land? Better than the Garden of Eden, they said.

Any treasure? Some Indians had headdresses made of solid gold.

How about the people? Friendly.

They had been invited to dinner at a chief's home, they reported. Before they ate, the women took off all the men's clothes, washed them, dried them, and helped the men get dressed again. Where in England would they receive such treatment?

The queen was so excited at the news that she knighted Walter Raleigh. Now he was Sir Walter, the owner of the queen's seven-year patent to settle land in the New World.

Sir Walter was so excited that he named the new English land Virginia in honor of Elizabeth, the virgin queen. Right away he began planning the next trip. This time he would send Sir Richard Grenville, Amadas, and Barlow, with Ralph Lane as second in command.

On April 9, 1585, seven ships sailed from England. On board were five hundred men and two dogs—giant mastiffs trained for fighting. Also present were two Indians whom Amadas and Barlow had brought back to England as part of their show-and-tell report. One of them was Manteo, who fell in love with England; the other was Wanchese, who hated England on sight.

The plan was for Sir Richard Grenville to stay with the colonists and return to England later for more men and supplies.

In his absence Ralph Lane would give the orders, especially orders about what to do in case they ran into hostile Indians. Never turn the other cheek, they were told. No, they should smite such people. Smite them hip and thigh. Smite them to death, if need be.

At the end of July they reached land and anchored off Cape Hatteras, that long arm of land that wraps itself around the islands as if to prevent them from drifting out to sea. Almost immediately Indians from a nearby village came swarming over the ships. Although they were friendly, they were not wearing gold headdresses or anything else made of gold. Just as the English were thinking treasure, however, so were the Indians. As they looked around, what they saw was a small silver cup. What they did was take it. It was not until after the Indians had left that the English noticed the silver cup was missing. It was not something they valued highly, but it was *theirs*. Amadas was put in charge of eleven men and ordered to go into the village and bring the cup back.

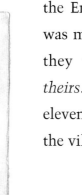

NEW WORLD

Cape Hatteras

ATLANTIC OCEAN

VIRGINIA

Roanoke Island

Cape Hatteras

What cup? the Indians asked.

Time for smiting, hip and thigh, the English decided. So hip and thigh, they burned down all the crops in the village. Hip and thigh, they set the houses on fire.

When the men returned to the ships (without the silver cup), it was time to go ashore. But this was not easy. Roanoke Island was situated in shallow water among shoals and sandbanks. It was a hard place to reach. The flagship, the *Tiger*, which carried most of their food supplies, struck a shoal. For eleven hours waves pounded the boat and washed over the deck, threatening the lives of all on board, soaking their food supply. Eventually they were able to free the *Tiger*. The men were safe, but what about their food? A soggy diet lay ahead.

Sir Richard Grenville

When everyone was finally ashore, including the two mastiffs, they began to set up their colony. They started with a fort on the north end of the island so that they could feel safe, especially if the Spanish came. Then they built their houses—small, two-story wooden houses with grass-covered roofs. The houses for the officers and "gentlemen" were placed outside the fort, but those for the common soldiers were inside. A larger structure was used as a storehouse. Since the island was only about ten miles long and three miles wide, they were satisfied to build only what was necessary. But it would have been nice to have a proper harbor to get in and out of quickly in case they sighted Spanish treasure ships.

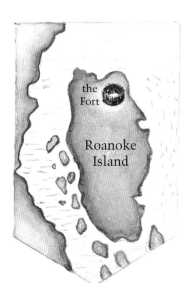

the Fort

Roanoke Island

the Fort

Manteo

Wingina

After about seven weeks, Sir Richard Grenville left for England, promising to come back soon with food. Ralph Lane was glad to be rid of him. Grenville was a difficult man with a quick temper. No matter how vile the weather or how wormy the food, Grenville had insisted on eating on his gold or silver plates. But Lane had personal reasons for disliking Grenville. Once in the Caribbean when Grenville had asked for advice from his officers, Lane had made a suggestion that so angered Grenville, he threatened to put Lane on trial for his life. Of course Lane was happy to see Grenville leave. He would go exploring.

He divided his men into two groups. His group (forty men and two dogs) went up the Roanoke River in search of a copper mine. When they returned to Roanoke, they had not found a copper mine or anything else of value.

The second group went to the Chesapeake Bay area, spent most of the winter, and reported that the land around the bay would make a fine place for a settlement. The soil was fertile, the climate pleasant, and the people friendly. The only thing it lacked was a proper harbor. So far, they hadn't found one.

Next, Lane's men began taking trips in small boats up the Chowan River, stopping frequently to visit with Indians along the way. Much of the time they were fed. Sometimes Manteo, the Indian who loved England and had learned English, was with them and acted as interpreter. If he was not along, they tried to talk with their hands. Often they made friends with Indians, but sometimes they made enemies.

Once they met an Indian who lived on the island, and they asked his name. He replied, "Wingina," and then said, "Wingandoca." The English thought that "Wingina" was his name and that "Wingandoca" was the place where he lived. What he was really telling them was that "Wingina" was the name of the king of the Secotan tribe, who lived on Roanoke Island. Moreover, he was giving the English a compliment. "You wear nice clothes," he said. In any case, he made friends with the English, gave them food, and stayed with them, even adopting their religion.

In their travels, Thomas Hariot wrote down all that they saw; John White, well known for his watercolors, drew all that he saw; and they all listened to stories of treasure. There was a place, they were told, where there were large supplies of both copper and pearls.

Where was this place?

No one had a satisfactory answer until they had gone about 110 miles farther on the mainland to the headquarters of Menatonon, king of the Choanokes. He was an old man and crippled, but in two days he gave them more information about the countryside than they had received anywhere along the way. And yes, he knew the place that had both copper and pearls. To get there would take three days by canoe, followed by four days on land. Anyone who went should have many men, for the king of that place did not like strangers.

Lane was suspicious. Was this the truth?

Menatonon gave Lane a rope of black pearls and offered to supply him with guides if he wanted them.

Menatonon

9

Even now, Lane was not sure if he could trust the old king. To be certain, he kidnapped the king's favorite son, put him in handcuffs, and later, when he tried to run away, fastened irons on his legs. Still, the Roanoke explorers were not quite ready to go home. They had a little copper to trade for food, as they had been doing all along.

But as they went on, there was no one to trade with. The country was empty, as though the woods had swallowed all signs of life. A few small fires burned on the shore, but whoever had started them had vanished.

The men were hungry, *very* hungry. They tried eating sassafras leaves, but that was worse than not eating at all. Then one morning they ate the dogs' porridge and let the dogs go hungry. The next day they ate the dogs.

Then they went home, hoping to find that Grenville had returned with food and supplies. They arrived at Roanoke on Easter and found nothing but bad news. Everyone was hungry. There was no sign of Grenville. Moreover, Wingina had taken everyone from his village and moved to the mainland.

Was he tired of Englishmen begging for food? The Indians didn't have enough food to be able to share. Perhaps Wingina was just simply tired of the English.

According to Menatonon's son, who had made friends with the local Indians, Wingina had called a meeting with neighboring tribes. Together they could starve the English out or simply kill them. Ralph Lane pictured it: They would set his house on fire and then they would "knock his brains" out. So he decided to take action while he still had his brains.

He would lead a surprise night attack on Wingina, and because no one could see in the dark, he told his men to pull out their white shirttails and let them hang loose. Don't shoot at shirttails, he warned. They didn't. The English came through unharmed, but Wingina was dead.

The battle was over. Still, everyone was hungrier than ever. Lane divided the men into small groups, sent them to different locations, and told them to live off the land. Eat fish, crabs, berries. Whatever. And keep a sharp lookout for ships. Surely Sir Richard Grenville would come soon.

One of Lane's officers, Captain Stafford, went to Croatan, Manteo's hometown, about forty miles across the water on Cape Hatteras. He had been there for about three weeks when he saw a large fleet of twenty-three sails approaching.

Were these Spanish ships coming to drive the English from the land they had claimed for themselves?

Was it Grenville?

Stafford rushed to warn Lane.

As it turned out, it was Sir Francis Drake, England's most daring seaman, famous for his attacks on Spanish ships. Returning from an expedition in the Caribbean, he was stopping at Roanoke to see how

the new colony was doing. From raids on Spanish forts in Florida, he had collected things that might be useful to the colony—doors, windows, doorknobs. He also brought with him 250 black slaves to help with the work.

Drake took his fleet up the Roanoke River, and when he and Lane met, he offered the people a choice. If they wanted to stay in Roanoke longer, he would give them a supply of food and a good-sized boat to take them back to England. If they wanted to leave soon, he would take them with him.

Lane wanted to stay. He had one more job, one more exploration to make. He wanted to find that harbor on Chesapeake Bay, and he was pleased that his men felt the same way. They would stay, he told Drake.

But as he spoke, dark clouds gathered on the southern horizon. A storm was coming, but what of it? They had seen storms before; they had even weathered hurricanes.

But this was no ordinary hurricane. It came roaring in the next day as if it had a particular grudge against this part of the world, as if it had been saving up its anger so that it could show once and for all just how violent weather could be. Roaring, the sky hurled down hailstones as big as cannonballs. The ocean reared up and crashed down, foaming in a kind of mad orgy, spitting up waterspouts, dragging boats out to sea. What could mere men do in the midst of such fury except pray that it end? It went on for three days.

When it was over, the men, and Lane himself, wanted only to get out of there. Take us back to England, they begged Drake. Now. Quickly.

Drake agreed. He sent his sailors into Roanoke to alert the settlers who were still there. "Come on!" the sailors cried. "Bring your baggage, only *hurry!*"

They piled into whatever little boats they could find. There were so many of them and the sea was still so rough that the boats rocked, threatening to turn over. The sailors began throwing the baggage into the water. Everything. John White's drawings. The rope of black pearls that Menatonon had given Ralph Lane.

Even the string of perfect white pearls meant for the queen.

They were in such an all-fired rush when they set sail, they forgot about the three men who were still out exploring.

Although no one knew it, Sir Richard Grenville was on his way to Roanoke from England at that very moment. When he arrived, he found the colony deserted. What was going on? What had happened to everyone?

When Grenville finally sailed back to England after spending two weeks in the empty colony, he left fifteen men behind to hold the island for the English.

What was he thinking? How could fifteen men survive, especially when most of the Indians had gone through a year of hip-and-thigh treatment?

Settling

Of course Sir Walter Raleigh was disappointed that his colonists had turned tail and run because of a storm, no matter how bad it was. He also worried about the rumors that Spain was getting ready to attack England. And there was a rumor in the palace that Walter was writing love poems to a lady-in-waiting to the queen. Perhaps the queen hadn't heard this rumor, but if she had, she wouldn't have liked it any more than she liked hearing about Spain's plans.

In any case, Sir Walter was not going to give up on his colony. He would send out a new expedition, but this one would be different. It would be a permanent colony made up not just of soldiers, but of families willing to settle there for life. It would not be at Roanoke, which had only brought bad luck. Of course, they would have to go to Roanoke first to pick up the fifteen men Grenville had left there. Then they would go on to find their permanent site on Chesapeake Bay. Here they would build what would be called the "Cittie of Raleigh."

Sir Walter Raleigh

(Sir Walter loved the sound of it.) Sir Walter appointed John White, a member of the first expedition, to be governor and gave him a council of twelve men.

Sir Walter offered 500 free acres of land to anyone who agreed to be a settler. John White, who was already familiar with the land, knew this was a promise that could be kept only if all the Indians were wiped out. Besides, no settler could hope to cultivate more than five acres unless his farm came equipped with oxen, horses, plows, and maybe a couple of miracles.

Some couples may have been persuaded by the acreage. But not John White's daughter, Eleanor White Dare, or her husband, Ananais Dare. Eleanor had grown up hearing stories from her father about how wonderful America was. Now she would settle there. When the Cittie of Raleigh grew to full size, her father would be living in the governor's mansion. Since her mother was not living, Eleanor must have planned to be at her father's side, keeping him company, helping to

Eleanor Dare

Ananais Dare

entertain important visitors. The fact that she was pregnant as they started their journey didn't seem to bother Eleanor. She'd be in her own home when the baby arrived.

On the twenty-sixth of April, 1587, three ships left England for Virginia. Packed with citizens eager to build the new Cittie of Raleigh, there were eighty-seven men, seventeen women, and eleven children, which included fourteen families. Only one person was unwelcome to the settlers.

Simon Fernandez, the Portuguese pilot-navigator, wanted everything his way. More interested in privateering than in collecting supplies, he took "the golden highway" through the Caribbean, the common route for Spanish treasure ships. He was supposed to get supplies for the settlement as they went along, but he frustrated John White at every turn. He couldn't find the sheep he was supposed to pick up. The friend who was going to supply them with cattle was not there. The supply of salt seemed to be nonexistent. Sometimes it must have seemed to the colonists that Fernandez was deliberately trying to subvert the colony, but why would he do that? He had bought a share in the venture for himself.

On July 16 they finally started north for Virginia, but Simon Fernandez was so confused (or pretended to be) that he mistook Cape Fear in North Carolina for Manteo's home, Croatan, on Cape Hatteras. Had it not been for the interference of Captain Stafford, Fernandez would have run his ship aground and cast away the whole company. And when they finally reached Roanoke Island, what did Fernandez do?

Simon Fernandez

He simply ignored Sir Walter's instructions. He didn't pick up the fifteen men that Grenville had left behind, and he didn't sail directly to Chesapeake Bay to begin building their city as he was supposed to do.

As the colonists were landing on Roanoke, an unidentified gentleman, prompted by Fernandez, called out that this was as far as they were going. It was July 22, and it was too late in the season for planting, he said. They would all be left on Roanoke and would have to get along as well as they could.

What was John White to do?

Although he was governor, he did nothing. Perhaps he had simply learned that Master Simon Fernandez was not to be crossed nor was he to be trusted. According to John White, whatever Fernandez did was out of "meanness."

The settlers, however, were not ready to give up on Chesapeake Bay. But first, they had to set up some kind of day-to-day life on Roanoke Island. They examined the houses that Ralph Lane had left behind. They were still standing, but there were noises from inside. Were they already occupied?

Indians?

Grenville's men?

No. Deer. Pumpkin and melon vines were growing wild on the first floor of all the houses, and deer were gorging on them.

A ✦ River

B ✦ Cornfield
guard hut

C ✦ Homes

D ✦ Solemn feast
area

E ✦ Ripe corn

F ✦ Sunflowers

G ✦ Pumpkins

H ✦ Young corn

I ✦ Tobacco

J ✦ Prayer area

K ✦ Feasting area

L ✦ Celebration
area

M ✦ Tomb for
kings and
princes

*Engravings of a typical Indian village and some of its possible inhabitants,
based on John White watercolors.*

Governor White ordered the houses to be cleared and new ones to be built for the families with them. And what about Grenville's men? The bones of one man were found, but what of the others?

And what of George Howe, one of their own members, who had wandered off by himself after arriving at Roanoke? Wading in the water, Howe was fishing with a forked stick for crab when he was shot by Indians hiding behind him. He was shot sixteen times, and then had his head beaten into bits.

The next day, Governor John White and some of his officers went to Manteo's village, Croatan, to find answers to some of their questions.

Yes, Manteo's people knew about Grenville's men. Eleven had escaped by boats, but to where? They didn't know.

John White suggested that the Croatans gather the leaders of the towns who had killed George Howe and bring them in seven days' time to Roanoke for a peace conference.

The seven days came and went, and when no one showed up, Governor White, sounding like Ralph Lane, said it was time to teach the Indians a lesson.

He led an attack at midnight, but they could barely see what they were doing. In the morning it turned out they had been fighting Manteo's friendly tribe, not enemies.

What could the English say? They were sorry.

What else? On August 2, they held an official ceremony and made Manteo "Lord of Roanoke."

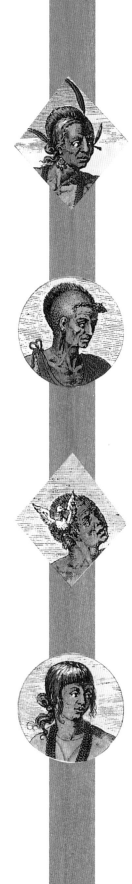

Two weeks later it was Eleanor Dare's turn to make history. On August 18 she gave birth to a girl, the first English child born in America. They named her Virginia, and the following week she was christened by her grandfather, Governor White.

Still, the settlers had done nothing about resupplying themselves not only with food, but with all the things they had counted on finding on their way.

Someone would have to go back to England and plead their case. The settlers asked each of the governor's assistants to take the job. All refused except Christopher Cooper, but the next day he changed his mind. Well, there was nothing to do, the settlers said, but to ask the governor himself to go. Perhaps secretly they worried about the governor's leadership abilities. He had never been able to stand up to Fernandez. If they decided to move to Chesapeake Bay, would the governor agree? In any case, he was in the best position to persuade Sir Walter of their needs and to explain how Fernandez had betrayed them. So all the men in the settlement went in a body to entreat John White to go to England and represent them.

Governor White refused. What would Sir Walter think of him, giving up as leader of the colony so soon?

Don't worry, the settlers said. They would write a letter telling Sir Walter how the governor had refused the job until they had insisted that he go.

Still, the governor said no. What would happen to all his possessions? He had brought pictures, books, and maps to decorate the governor's mansion. He had brought his best suit of armor.

The settlers promised to watch over them carefully. The next day they returned—all the settlers this time, not only the men but the women too. Even his daughter, Eleanor Dare.

John White could no longer resist their unanimous appeal.

But what if the settlers moved in his absence? the governor asked. Would they carve on a tree or post the name of the place they were going? They promised.

And if they were in danger, would they draw a cross over their message? Agreed.

And so, on the morning of the next day, August 27, 1587, the entire colony came to the water's edge to bid their governor farewell. Probably the last thing that John White did was to give his little granddaughter, Virginia, a hug. How he must have hated to leave her!

Then John White disappeared over the unpredictable sea, not able to imagine his future. Neither could the settlers imagine what lay ahead for them. All they knew was that they were alone. Alone in a wild new country.

Lost

John White hoped for a fair wind and smooth seas so he could get back to Roanoke in record time. But when had John White been lucky enough to have his wishes granted? The first thing that went wrong was that the capstan broke. The capstan was the large spool-like contraption on the deck around which the anchor rope was wound. In the process, an anchor was lost. But worse than that, as the capstan swung out of control, the rods that extended from it whirred around at such a dizzying speed, they hit anyone or anything in the way. Five men were hit, two wounded seriously. This meant that instead of fifteen men, only ten men were left to run the governor's ship. Some of these sickened, some died. Even the sky looked sick, as if it might not last the journey. For six days John White and his men wandered in a gray world with neither the sun visible by day nor the stars by night. Where were they?

On October 16 they saw land, but they didn't know they were on the west coast of Ireland. Fortunately, some Irish saw that they were in trouble and helped them to shore.

"You won't be going back to sea soon," the Irish told them.

Spain was at war with England, and Queen Elizabeth was keeping all her ships close to home.

When John White met Sir Walter in England, he heard the same story. He would just have to wait.

Wait! What about Roanoke Island? What about little Virginia Dare?

Five months later, in March 1588, Sir Richard Grenville was able to free a couple of his ships for the Roanoke trip, but at the last minute the queen canceled the order. More waiting. In April 1588, two small ships—pinnaces, built to navigate shallow waters—were assigned to Sir Walter. One ship was mainly for supplies, the other for the governor and the new colonists he had gathered for his city. With so many enemy vessels scouting about, several larger ships were ordered to escort the smaller ones bound for Roanoke. However, most of the time the large ones went their own way.

The small ships and their captains, on the other hand, didn't act as if they wanted chaperones. Once they were out at sea, they went wild, like children let out of school, looking for trouble. Every sail they saw, they chased, no matter how large the ship, no matter what country owned it.

Of course it was foolhardy to attack a large, well-equipped French ship, and of course they came to regret it. The French sailors wasted no time. Boarding the English ships, they did battle with all whom they saw, injuring both the captain and the first mate so seriously, they were unable to get out of bed. Governor White did not escape. His head was bashed with both a sword and a pike. A bullet hit him in the buttocks, so he had trouble sitting down. The French did not let up, determined, it seemed, on killing every last Englishman. At last their captain intervened. He agreed to call off the fight if the English would not only surrender, but say so.

The English did. They would have said anything to stop the killing. They watched the French strip their decks of everything movable, anything useful.

And Roanoke? Who but Governor White gave Roanoke a thought?

Sir Walter tried again to send help to his foundering colony. He loaded a small pinnace with emergency supplies, but it was never allowed to leave England. 1588 was the year the Spanish Armada attacked England, so the English were far too busy to help settlers in trouble on the other side of the Atlantic Ocean.

By 1590 the fighting was over and seagoing Englishmen were longing to return to the Caribbean. Ships were cleaned and gathered on the Thames and at southern ports. Among them were two that

would participate in privateering, but were specifically assigned to relieve the Virginia Colony—the *Moonlight* with Captain Spicer and the *Hopewell* with Captain Edward C. Cocke.

Of course, Governor White, along with a group of new settlers, expected to go, but at the last minute the settlers were stopped. They would not be allowed, they were told. No extra people. The ship was too crowded. Moreover, the governor would be permitted to take only one chest. "And not even a boy to tend me!" the governor complained. He might have carried his objections to Sir Walter, but perhaps he was afraid that even he might be denied passage.

On March 20, the ships left England. They reached the Caribbean without incident, and then began months of chasing around the islands.

The English did manage to capture several small prizes and one large cargo ship so rich, it could have paid for three English ships of war. But Governor White was restless. All those wasted months in the Caribbean! Waiting without end.

When they finally reached the vicinity of Roanoke, the governor would surely have gone to the prow of the ship, his eyes scanning the scene. It was so familiar—the islands strewn behind the cape as if they had been tossed there haphazardly. And his colonists—Virginia Dare too—on one of those islands. Would they see him coming and rush to the shoreline? No, but they might send a signal. Governor White and Captain Cocke noticed a plume of smoke rising from the far end of the island.

They passed through an inlet of the cape, but ahead lay the treacherous waters around Roanoke. Ahead lay the shoal that ran beside the land and had caused so much trouble in the past. When the wind was just right (from the northeast), it swept up the water into mountainous waves that broke on the bar, putting into peril any ships in the way.

The wind was just right as the *Moonlight* and the *Hopewell* came to the bar. Fortunately, Captain Cocke had a skillful pilot who rode the waves and brought the *Hopewell* safely to land. Not so with the *Moonlight*. The water rose up into a wall, then broke over the ship, capsizing it. Eleven men were on board. Captain Spicer and one of his crew tried hanging on to the sides of the ship, but the waves were too much for them. Others tried wading to shore, but they too were overcome.

Captain Cocke, however, was a strong swimmer. He stripped off

his clothes and, along with several other good swimmers, went to the rescue. They managed to save four sailors. But not Captain Spicer. Not any of the six others.

Eventually they were able to turn the *Moonlight* right side up, but that was all any of the sailors were willing to do. Enough was enough, they said.

They were determined to go home.

No, Captain Cocke replied firmly. He pointed to the smoke still rising in the distance. They were going to investigate. Perhaps the colonists who had come here three years ago were signaling them.

It was night when they reached the fire, and too dark to leave the ship. So they tied up onshore and Captain Cocke ordered the trumpeter to sound while all those on the ship called out, as they said, "Friendly." But no one responded; no one came running to the ship. Apparently they needed more assurance that these were really English friends. The men began singing familiar English songs—sea songs, love songs, hymns. Their voices hung in the still night air of the wilderness as if they were calling the colonists home. Behind the smoke, there was no sound, no activity, no sing-along, no amens at the end of hymns.

In the first light of morning, the English went to see for themselves. There was nothing to see. No one to talk to. All that smoke simply came from rotten trees and grass burning. The only sign of life was the bare footprints of passing Indians who must have wondered at the sound of English voices in their woods.

Looking farther on the island, Governor White noted that all the houses he had left standing were gone. Among the tall weeds, pieces of metal (including four cannon) were scattered as if they had been considered useless or too heavy to transport. Roanoke was deserted.

The colonists had obviously moved. Where? Three letters were carved on a tree: CRO. That was all.

Farther on, at a more conspicuous place at the entry of the fort, the entire word was spelled out: CROATAN. This was the home of their friend Manteo and his tribe. Well then, the governor reasoned, his people were safe, particularly as there was no cross above CROATAN indicating that they had left in danger.

It was clear that Indians had made themselves at home on the island. The three chests that White had left in the care of the colonists had been dug up and the contents damaged, most beyond repair. His books had the covers torn off; the pages had been ruined by weather. The frames around his maps and pictures had been destroyed, and as for his armor (which one would think the Indians would have liked, if only for the metal), it was discarded and rusted through.

The governor and Captain Cocke decided that they would go to Croatan the next day for a grand reunion with the colony. They took for granted that the weather wouldn't stop them. They should have known better. A storm developed overnight and took two cables and two anchors, which meant that they could anchor neither at Croatan nor at Roanoke. Their first thought was to return to the Caribbean for the winter and come back to the Roanoke area in the spring. Again, the weather had its way. No sooner had they set sail than they were turned north by the current. Willy-nilly they were headed for England. Willy-nilly they were leaving the settlers behind. Somewhere.

The *Hopewell* arrived in Plymouth in the south of England on October 24, but had nothing good to report. They had not found the colonists. The news spread over the country. Raleigh's colony had been lost. One hundred and fifteen people!

Clues

It is still hard for Americans to look at the country's history and see that hole right at the very beginning. And after more than four hundred years that hole is still there, although we are still looking just as we always have.

In 1600, the age of Queen Elizabeth was coming to an end. She had won her war with Spain, but she had failed to establish the first English colony in the New World. Not everyone, however, had given up on that colony. Certainly Sir Walter had not given up. He sent two ships to Roanoke. One went too far and found itself at Cape Fear. One did not go far enough and only got as far as Maine. Both returned to London.

In 1603 Elizabeth died and James, son of Mary Queen of Scots, came down from Scotland to be England's new monarch. James was interested in colonies too, and in 1607 Jamestown, the first permanent colony in America, was established.

But there was one thing about America that James couldn't abide. People returning from America brought with them supplies of Indian tobacco and Indian pipes. So now it was fashionable for young men all over England to go about sucking on pipes, blowing clouds of smoke about the land, sometimes right under King James's nose.

"Phew, phew," he would say, and make a nasty face to show how he hated the smell. Most men smoked pipes made out of nutshells with straws for stems, but Sir Walter had a silver pipe with a long silver stem. King James saved his nastiest face for Sir Walter.

King James knew about the Lost Colony at Roanoke. If there were

survivors, King James supposed they smoked too. But smokers or not, he wanted to find them. He ordered the new colonists at Jamestown to search for the old ones. And they did.

John Smith, the most adventurous of the colonists, picked up more clues than anyone else. One directly from Powhatan, chief of the Indian tribe living near Jamestown. He said that the lost colonists had been massacred by his own men. He even showed Smith some of the weapons they had used.

Smith, however, didn't report this except perhaps confidentially to the king. Indeed, it was ten years before this news was generally known.

There were other clues. George Percy, a member of the Jamestown colony, noticed a large plot of empty ground in the Chesapeake area that looked as if it might have been newly turned over—was this a cover to hide something? Percy never found out.

Meanwhile, John Smith sent two expeditions into the interior. They heard from Indians that there were two white men, four boys, and a maid working as slaves in a copper mine run by an Indian leader. Were these colonists who had escaped Powhatan's massacre? The explorers didn't find out; they didn't even see the slaves. Nobody did. They weren't allowed to be seen. For whatever reason, the English didn't try to rescue them.

Someone else reported seeing a yellow-haired boy, but he ran off before he was questioned.

A tribe of bearded Indians was reported. But Indians didn't have beards. Were they lost colonists? Again, no questions.

At this time there was little or no news about the lost colonists. It wasn't long before King James was dead (1625), but not until he had made sure that England was rid of Walter Raleigh. James had never

liked Sir Walter, but not even a king killed a man just because he smoked. Raleigh had more serious offenses. James claimed that Raleigh had plotted against him. So James did what kings in that day often did. He sent Raleigh to the Tower of London, and eventually he was beheaded.

John White had long since given up on the colony. He committed the settlers to God's mercy, he said, and left it at that. Not everyone, however, was willing to leave it at that.

The most believable story the English heard about the Lost Colony was Powhatan's story about the mass murder. But believable or not, the English did not believe it. If it had happened so long ago, why hadn't they heard it before? they asked. Why hadn't John Smith written it down? He never had. It was generally accepted that the colonists had divided into two parties—some going into the interior, some to Croatan.

The English were convinced that at least some of the lost colonists were still alive. Many from Jamestown had seen crosses carved on trees, indicating that Christians had been there. And what about the initials on a tree in the Blue Ridge Mountains? "M.A. and N.J."? Couldn't they stand for lost colonists Morris Allen and Nicolas Johnson? Of course, they could also stand for people before or after the lost colonists. This is not a convincing clue.

Meanwhile, the colony of North Carolina had grown so quickly that its people wanted to know more about it. So, in 1703 they employed

John Lawson to make a survey. Traveling by foot in remote areas, he was alert to any suggestions he might hear about the lost colonists. There were none until he reached Cape Hatteras and the Croatan Indians. "Yes," they said, "they had ancestors who dressed like you, and like you they could make books speak." (They meant "read.") There was no specific information about when the colonists had come to Croatan or how long they had stayed, but their story fit the message on the tree. Furthermore, John Lawson noted a number of Croatans who had gray eyes.

Time passed. A lot of time. Then, in 1937 a grocer from California made a trip to North Carolina and stirred up the mystery again. Walking beside a swamp one day, he stumbled on a large stone. It was not the kind of stone usually found in marshes and, moreover, this one had marks on it. The grocer, A. E. Hammond, washed the stone in a river and discovered it had readable letters: *Ananias Dare + Virginia went hence unto Heaven 1591.* On the other side was carved: *Anye Englishman shew John White gov Via.*

Realizing that he had discovered something important, Hammond took the stone to professors at Emory University in Atlanta. Very excited, the professors advertised that they would pay for any more stones that were found.

Money for stones? Of course more stones were found. In the end there was a total of forty-eight stones. Eleanor White Dare had her name on some of the stones, as she filled in the story of the colony. All colonists, save seven, were murdered, she wrote. The professors decided to buy the hill where the graves were supposedly located, but after a thorough search, they found nothing. According to the stones, Eleanor married a native chief and had a daughter, Agnes. On the last stone before she died, she begged her father to take Agnes to England.

Seeking a reputable authority, the professors invited the well-known historian Samuel Eliot Morison to examine the stones. He looked them over carefully. Yes, he said, they did appear to be authentic. Not all the names of the dead were on White's list, but they might have used nicknames, the professors suggested.

Eventually, the professors submitted the stones to further tests. Modern stonecutters agreed they could carve similar letters with simple tools such as those early colonists might have had.

But when the professors sought information on Hammond, they found nothing. Eventually they discovered that Hammond and two of the other stone finders had been longtime friends. Of course, this raised their suspicions. So they took the stones to an Elizabethan scholar, who dismissed them entirely. There was not a Gothic letter on the stones and Elizabethans wrote in Gothic script, if they wrote at all. All the letters were in Roman capitals, a style that only a highly educated Elizabethan would know. The scholar, however, had a trump card that settled the matter once and for all. The words *primeval* and *reconnoiter* had not even entered the English language at the time of the Roanoke colony. The stones were a hoax. They didn't solve a thing.

Yet the Lost Colony was still a mystery in America's imagination. Were there descendants? If so, where would they be?

Gothic
ROMAN

Raleigh
Ralegh
Rawley
Raulie
Rawlegh
Rawleighe
Raleghe
Rawlye
Rawleie
Rawligh
Raileigh
Raughlie
Rauleigh
Raleighe
Raghley
Raghlie
Ralleyghe
Ralighe
Raule
Rawlee
Rauley
Rawleye
Raulyghe
Rawlyghe
Rawlighe
Rauleighe
Raughlie

A group of Indians in Robeson County, North Carolina, claim to be descended from the lost colonists. After all, if the colonists had divided into two groups, as many people thought, some must have been assimilated with Indians. Some who migrated into the interior settled on the Lumber River. They called themselves Lumbees. After years of arguing with the U.S. government, they were finally recognized as Indians, but not as a separate tribe. In the first place, they spoke only English; they had no language of their own. Nor did they have any rituals that they practiced as other tribes did. Furthermore, they claimed that forty-one of the ninety-five surnames of the colonists were in use by the Lumbees. Spelling was so erratic at that time that the names might vary in spelling. (Raleigh's name, for instance, could be spelled over seventy different ways.)

Today most historians dismiss the connection of the Lumbees with the Lost Colony. They say they are simply a mixture of Sioux, Tuscarora, and perhaps Cherokee, with an obvious addition of white and black blood. The Lumbees themselves may not say much about their heritage, but not all deny it either. George Lowrie, of a famous outlaw family, says, "We were a free people long before the white man came to our land. Our tribe lived in Roanoke. There is white man's blood in these veins as well as that of the Indians."

How long can Americans keep up their curiosity about the Lost Colony? Indefinitely, perhaps. In the year 2001 a young anthropologist, Lee Miller, claimed to have "solved" the mystery of the lost colonists. She simply laid out the pieces of the puzzle in front of her, she said, and there, plain as day, was the story.

Why were they lost in the first place? she asked. It is hard for anyone who reads the story not to wonder about the subversive behavior of Simon Fernandez. How could he abandon the colonists on his own authority—simply out of "meanness," as John White contended? Lee Miller decided that someone of consequence must have been behind the plot, directing Simon Fernandez. Going through the state papers of the leading men under Queen Elizabeth, she eliminated them one by one until she came to Sir Francis Walsingham, secretary of state to the queen.

He had a record of not only manipulating events himself, but of employing spies to help him in his most daring ventures. After all, over a number of years he had secretly arranged for the downfall of

Rawlighe
Rauleighe
Raughlie
Rallegh
Rawlei
Rauly
Raughly
Raylye
Rolye
Rolle
Raleikk
Rale
Ralego
Rahlegh
Raley
Raleye
Raleagh
Raleyghe
Ralli
Raweleigh
Raylygh
Reigley
Rhaly
Wrawley
Ralo
Raulaeus
Raleghus

Mary Queen of Scots until at last she was tried in an illegal court and beheaded. If he could do this, why couldn't he arrange to lose a colony of new settlers?

Why would he want to? At this time Walsingham had at least 500 spies on his private payroll, which put him deeply in debt. He hoped Queen Elizabeth would help him, but she didn't. He expected her to turn over to him a part of the huge estate of Anthony Babbington, who had been caught in a plot to assassinate Queen Elizabeth. After he was hanged, Queen Elizabeth had to dispose of Babbington's estate. She gave it to Raleigh. This was the last straw for Walsingham. Still, there was that seven-year patent on new land in America that Sir Walter Raleigh held. If Raleigh's new colony failed, his patent would expire, and if Walsingham played his cards right, why couldn't the patent be his? Many people disliked Sir Walter because of his blasted pride. Sir Francis hated him.

Walsingham's plot seemed airtight. He had every reason to believe that Simon Fernandez would obey his instructions. Why wouldn't he? He owed his life to Sir Francis. A Portuguese, he had been captured at sea and taken to London to be hanged, but at the last minute Sir Francis Walsingham had interceded. Simon was set free. In time, he married an English girl, settled down in England, and must have become one of Sir Francis's spies. If he carried out his assignment against the colonists, he would be rewarded with far more money than he could have made as one of the governor's assistants. The colonists themselves must have suspected that Simon was carrying out orders from above. They may have been in fear for their own lives if they

went back to England, so they
insisted that the governor, who
had more clout, go.

Lee Miller claims to have solved
the mystery, but she cannot come up with proof. Neither
Walsingham nor Simon confessed, nor were there witnesses
who had anything to say. Still, Lee Miller has done extensive

research and has made an astute guess. Most important, she has given our story a villain.

Walsingham played no part in the rest of the story, nor did he profit from the colony's failure. He died before the first search party left for Roanoke (1590).

After the colonists left Roanoke, then what? When Lee Miller tells the story, it is no longer "as plain as day." Right from the beginning she insists that the colonists were not dead, but she has little to add to the story that was not known in 1608. She assumes that the colonists were in a war, were defeated, and as prisoners, they were used as slaves to work in an Indian copper mine. There may have been other prisoner-slaves in other parts of the state, according to a map made by John Smith, but the Indians would not allow any communication with the English. So the mystery remains.

One group of colonists has been left out. How about those who indicated they were going to Croatan? The consensus is that women

and children were in this group (certainly Eleanor and Virginia Dare) and perhaps a few men. They took refuge with the Croatans while the rest of the colonists struck off for the interior.

Dr. David Phelps, director of the East Carolina University coastal archaeology program, believes that clues may turn up underground. Every spring for a number of years he has gone with his team to the location where the Croatans once lived (present-day Buxton, North Carolina) and dug extensive trenches, carefully examining every few inches of sand so nothing will be missed.

So far nothing specifically related to the Lost Colony has turned up. In the year 2000 a gold signet ring stamped with a prancing lion was uncovered; this was significant since many signet rings had been found in Jamestown, but all had been made of brass. But this was gold, indicating it had been owned by a man of some prominence. A copy of the ring's design was sent to an Elizabethan expert in England. The report came back that it had belonged to a member of the Kendall family. One member had been part of Lane's colony. Another Kendall (a relative perhaps) was the captain of one of Drake's ships that had rescued Lane and his men in 1586. This was not the time of the Lost Colony, but it was close. Along with Lane's party, Kendall left Roanoke (without his ring) in 1586. John White left Roanoke in 1587, and no one in his colony was ever seen or heard from again. At least not by any English person. Of course, we may find more clues. We know, however, that this is not only a mystery; it is a tragic story.

And who is to blame for the tragedy?

Ralph Lane (without a doubt), who so alienated the Indians, there could be little hope of friendly relations with a future colony.

Indians (perhaps) who may have captured and made slaves of some colonists.

Sir Francis Walsingham (probably), an official in Queen Elizabeth's court.

Simon Fernandez (certainly), the Portuguese pilot of the expedition.

And yes, the weather. Always the weather, for it had a habit of whipping up a storm at every critical moment.

So it remains a mystery. And unless some new evidence turns up, we will just have to wonder.

Notes

Page 3 • Whether or not Raleigh actually tossed his coat over a mud puddle is not documented, but the story has become attached to him. It is the kind of gallant gesture he would have made, especially with the queen.

Page 4 • Dr. Dee's "show stone" must have been familiar with Spanish charts that showed Roanoke and Cape Hatteras, 36° north latitude. In Queen Elizabeth's time all of this area in the patent was Virginia. Not until 1691 did North Carolina become a separate colony with its own governor.

Page 8 • The English brought a great quantity of copper with them for trading purposes. Indians had little metal, so they welcomed the copper.

Page 10 • If the country was empty, it is probably because the Indian population fell victim to European diseases (especially smallpox), which were often fatal.

Page 13 • The slaves were not allowed off Drake's ship at Roanoke. There is no account of what happened to them.

Page 20 • The difference between a privateer and a pirate: A privateer had the permission and license from the queen to attack another ship, but must also give the queen a percentage of the profit; a pirate was on his own.

Page 20 • Simon Fernandez had once sailed these waters with Raleigh's half brother, Sir Humphrey Gilbert. His expertise was respected. His word always seemed to be final.

Page 23 • It was not a spur-of-the-moment idea to make Manteo "Lord of Roanoke." Sir Walter Raleigh had ordered that this be done before they left England. This was a good time to do it.

Page 30 ✦ The Spanish Armada refers to the fleet of 130 Spanish ships with 300,000 men sent to invade England. Sometimes it was called the Invincible Armada because the Spanish were so sure of winning. Instead, the English, aided by auspicious winds, chased the Spanish up the English Channel and around Scotland. The Spanish never managed to invade England, and when they went home, they had only half their fleet.

Page 40 ✦ In a war, Indians often took prisoners and made them slaves.

Page 41 ✦ This was not the only time Raleigh was imprisoned in the Tower of London. In July 1592, when the queen heard that Raleigh had secretly married Bess Throckmorton, her lady-in-waiting, she sent both Raleigh and Bess to the Tower. This was not too severe. They were allowed to take their servants, who could cook for them and for any guests they might invite. After four months Raleigh and Bess were released from prison, but Raleigh was not allowed to go to court for five years. During this time Raleigh was the victim of all kinds of slander: He was called an atheist, a freethinker, ambitious, covetous. His enemies, including King James, were determined to bring him down.

Bibliography

Bradley, A. G. *Captain John Smith*. New York: Macmillan, 1905.

Dial, Adolph. *The Lumbee*. New York: Chelsea House, 1993.

Hariot, Thomas. *A Brief and True Report of the New Found Land of Virginia* (1588). Ann Arbor: University of Michigan Microfilm.

Highwater, Jamake. *The Primal Mind*. New York: Harper, 1981.

Hume, Ivor Nöel. *The Virginia Adventure: Roanoke to James Towne*. New York: Knopf, 1994.

Kupperman, Karen. *Roanoke: The Abandoned Colony*. Totowa, N.J.: Rowman & Allanheld, 1984.

Melton, Frances Jones. "Croatons: The Lost Colony of America." *The Mid-continent Magazine* VI (July 1895): 195–202.

Miller, Lee. *Roanoke: Solving the Mystery of the Lost Colony*. New York: Arcade, 2001.

Morgan, Edmund. *American Slavery, American Freedom*. New York: Norton, 1975.

Powell, William S. "American Colonists and Explorers: An Attempt at Identification." *North Carolina Historical Review* XXXIV, vol. 2 (April 1957): 108–216.

Quinn, David Beers, ed. *The Roanoke Voyages*, vol. 1 & 2. New York: Dover, 1991.

Quinn, David Beers. *Set Fair for Roanoke: Voyages and Colonies, 1584–1606*. Chapel Hill: University of North Carolina Press, 1985.

Schouweiler, Tom. *The Lost Colony of Roanoke*. San Diego: Greenhaven, 1991.

Smith, Bradford. *Captain John Smith*. New York: Lippincott, 1953.

Sparkes, Boyden. "Writ on Rocke." *Saturday Evening Post*, April 26, 1941, 9–11.

Strachey, William. *The Historie of Travell into Virginia Britania* (1612). Edited by Louis B. Wright and Virginia Freund. London: The Hakluyt Society, 1953.

Index

A

Allen, Morris, 41
Amadas, Philip, 4, *4*, *5*, 6

B

Babbington, Anthony, 46
Barlow, Arthur, 4, *4*, *5*, 6
Blue Ridge Mountains, 41
Buxton, N.C., 49

C

Cape Fear, 20, 38
Cape Hatteras, 6, *6*, 12, 20, 42
Caribbean, 12, 30, 35
    "golden highway" of, 20
Cherokee, 44
Chesapeake Bay, 8, 13, 18, 21, 24, 40
Choanokes, 9
Chowan River, 8
Cittie of Raleigh, 18–19, 20
Cocke, Edward C., 31–33, 35
colonists:
    in arrival on Roanoke Island, 6–7
    bound for Chesapeake Bay, 18–21
    food needs and hunger of, 7, 8, 9,
        10–11, 13, 24
    see also Roanoke Island
Cooper, Christopher, 24

copper, 8, *9*, 10, 40, 48
Croatan, 12, 20, 23, 35, 41, 42, 48
Croatans (Indians), 23, 35, 42, 49
crosses carved on trees, 25, 35, 41

D

Dare, Ananais, 19, *19*, 42
Dare, Eleanor White, 19–20, *19*, 24, *24*, 25,
        42–43, 49
Dare, Virginia, 24, *24*, 25, 28, 32, 42, 49
Dee, Dr. John, 4
dogs, on first Roanoke expedition, 6, 7, 8, 10
Drake, Sir Francis, 12–14, *13*, 49
    raids on Spanish forts by, 13
    visit to Roanoke Colony by, 12–14

E

East Carolina University, 49
Elizabeth I, Queen of England, 2–3, *3*, 4, *5*, 18,
        29, 38, 45, *45*, 46
    and settling of New World, 2–4
    and war with Spain, 28–29
Elizabethan language, 43
Emory University, 42–43

F

Fernandez, Simon, 20–21, *20*, 50, *50*
    plotting by, 45, *45*, 46
Florida, 2, 13

food and hunger, 7, 8, *9*, 10–11, 13, 24
French ships, battles with, 29–30

G

gold, 2, 4, 6
"golden highway," in Caribbean, 20
gold signet ring, discovery of, 49, *49*
Gothic script, 43
Grenville, Sir Richard, 4, 6, 7, 8, 12, 28
    and abandoned colonists, 15, 18, 21, 23

H

Hammond, A. E., 42–43
Hariot, Thomas, 9, *9*
hoax, of North Carolina stones, 42–43, *42*
Hopewell, 31–33, 35
Howe, George, 23
Hudson River, 2

I

Indians, 33, 48, 49
    along Chowan River, 8–9
    attack on Howe by, 23
    Croatan, 23, 35, 42, 49
    early reports about, 4
    gold headdresses of, 4, 6
    in encounter with first Roanoke
        expedition, 6–7
    in Jamestown, 39–40
    pipes and tobacco of, 38–39
    of Robeson County, N.C., 44
Ireland, 28

J

James I, King of England, 38–39, *38*, 40–41
Jamestown, 38–39, 40, 41, 49
Johnson, Nicolas, 41

K

Kendall family, 49

L

Lane, Ralph, 4, 6, *6*, 8, 12–15, 21, 49, 50, *50*
    in attack on Wingina, 11
    in encounters with Indians, 8–11
Lawson, John, 42
"Lord of Roanoke" (Manteo), 23
Lowrie, George, 44
Lumbees, 44
Lumber River, 44

M

Maine, 38
Manteo, 6, 8, *8*, 12, 20, 23, 35
Mary Queen of Scots, 38, 46
Menatonon, 9, *9*, 11, 15
Miller, Lee, 44–48
Moonlight, 31–33
Morison, Samuel Eliot, 43

N

North Carolina, 20, 41–42
    stones discovered in, 42–43, *42*

P

pearls, 2, 9, 15
Percy, George, 40
Phelps, Dr. David, 49
Plymouth, England, 35
Powhatan, 39, *39*, 40, 41
privateering, 20, 31

R

Raleigh, Sir Walter, 2–4, *3*, *18*, 21, 24, 28, 31,
    38, *38*, 44, *45*, 46
    attempted voyages to Roanoke by, 29–30

imprisonment and beheading of, 41, *41*

knighting of, 4

second expedition sought by, 18–20

seven-year land patent of, 4, 46

Roanoke Island, 7, *7*

first expedition to, 6–15

Grenville's abandonment of colonists on, 15, 18, 21, 23

search for colonists on, 33–35, 38–42

second expedition to, 18–25

theories on lost colonists of, 38–51

third expedition to, 30–35

Roanoke River, 8, 13

Robeson County, N.C., Indians in, 44

Roman capitals, 43

S

Scotland, 38

Secotans, 9

Sioux, 44

slaves, transported by Drake, 13, *12–13*

Smith, John, 39–40, *39*, 41, 48

smoking, 38–39, 41

Spain, 2, 12, 18, 38

at war with England, 28–29, 30, 38

Spicer, Captain, 31–33

spying, 46, *47*

Stafford, Captain, 12, *12*, 20

stones, as alleged link to colonists, 42–43

storms, 13–15, 18, 35

T

Thames River, 30

Tiger, 7

tobacco, 38–39

Tower of London, 41, *41*

treasure, 2, 4, 6, 9, 20

trees, crosses carved on, 25, 35, 41

Tuscarora, 44

V

Virginia Colony, 20, 30

naming of, 4

W

Walsingham, Sir Francis, 45–48, *47*, 50, *50*

Wanchese, 6

weapons, of Jamestown Indians, 39, *39*

White, John, *8*, 9, 15, 24, 34, 41, 42, 45, 49

attack on Manteo's tribe by, 23

in attempts to reach Roanoke, 28–30

as governor of Roanoke Colony, 19–21

in return to England, 24–25

in return to Roanoke, 31–35

Wingandoca, 9

Wingina, *8*, 9

attack on, 11, *10–11*

JEAN FRITZ

Winner of a Newbery Honor and the National Book Award for her autobiographical book *Homesick*, Jean Fritz (1915–2017) wrote over forty highly acclaimed books for young readers, including *Leonardo's Horse*, which Hudson Talbott also illustrated. Her other titles include *And Then What Happened, Paul Revere?*; *Will You Sign Here, John Hancock?*; and *Shh! We're Writing the Constitution* for younger readers, and *Bully for You, Teddy Roosevelt!*; *Alexander Hamilton: The Outsider*; and *You Want Women to Vote, Lizzie Stanton?* for middle-graders.

Jean was awarded the National Humanities Medal in 2003 and is considered one of the top biographers for children.

HUDSON TALBOTT

Hudson Talbott has written and illustrated over twenty books, including *United Tweets of America: 50 State Birds*; *From Wolf to Woof: The Story of Dogs*; *It's All About Me-ow*; and *River of Dreams: The Story of the Hudson River*. He is the illustrator of *Leonardo's Horse*, also by Jean Fritz, and Newbery Honor winner *Show Way*, written by Jacqueline Woodson.

Hudson lives in New York City and the Hudson Valley.

www.hudsontalbott.com